T0131688

Spirit Songs, Images

AND

Uttered Nonsense

J. S. T. BOTTING

authorHOUSE®

AuthorHouse™
1663 Liberty Drive
Bloomington, IN 47403
www.authorhouse.com
Phone: 1 (800) 839-8640

Published by AuthorHouse 03/19/2020

ISBN: 978-1-7283-5173-5 (sc)
ISBN: 978-1-7283-5172-8 (e)

Library of Congress Control Number: 2020905317

Dedication

This book is dedicated to the many, many Muses I have met along the way who gave inspiration for my poetry.

I Would Not Speak

(A Concerto in Three Movements)

I would dance for you,
As the swirling leaves
Dance upon the forest floor,
Incited by the faerie sounds
Of the night wind's flute.
I would dance for you,
Among the scattered leaves,
Wearing only a veil
Of gossamer moonlight.
But, I would not speak.
There are no words
To express the passion
That leaps within my soul.

I would play for you,
As the breezes play,
Enchanting the forest
With the haunting strains
Of their ancient melody.
I would play for you,
Upon the lover's pipes,
Sweet lilting tunes
To capture the heart
And lure the timid spirit.
But, I would not speak.
I have no fluency
In spoken words
With which to enchant you.

I would touch you
As the gentle rays
Of a swelling moon
Stroke the naked trees,
A teasing warmth in the softness
Of their caress.
I would touch you thus,
To stir the embers
Of a primitive flame
That smolders deep inside.
But, I would not speak.
My words would only touch your mind.
I would not speak.
It is to the soul
That I would sing my spirit song.

Spirit Songs

Night Wind's Song

I will harness the mountain wind
And saddle it as a mare.
I'll braid a rope, for guiding rein,
From the golden summer flower.
I'll grace her shoulder with the moon,
To wear as jewel and brand,
And mount her on a starless night
To rise above the land.

I'll sit astride her back, as bold
As ever rider free,
And swiftly fly, across the sky,
To where you wait for me.
Thus, when you hear the night wind's song
Whisper in the trees
You'll know that it is I who rides
Mounted on the breeze.

If I Knew How

What if love should come along
And beckon me to go,
To rise up with the morn and walk
A path I do not know,
That, shadow cast, does quell the heart
Whose courage has grown thin,
And if I thought to acquiesce,
Where would I go from then?

And if I were to bravely rise
To face the dawning sun
And place my foot upon that path,
What then, once I've begun?
What hazards lie in wait for me,
Encouraged by my fear,
And who will answer when I cry,
Where do I go from here?

Oh, I could take that starting step
And another one, I think.
But, could my footsteps ever take me
Further than the brink?
And, once arriving at the edge, could
I find the strength to dare?
Yet, finding courage, still I ask,
Where would I go from there?

Where would I go from where I stand,
Fast rooted in dismay,
And what would happen to my heart
If I should lose my way?

Easy enough to live with dreams
That speak of love that heals
But, something different, yet again,
When all your dreams are real.

Comes now a new day with the sun
Scaling a soft-hued sky,
The winds that mutely held the night,
Exhaling with a sigh.
And I, awakening with the dawn,
Could, if I but knew how,
Seize this moment to be loved
But, where, of God, would I go from now?

The Woven Dreams of Man

My mind adrift, like listless clouds
That swirl and form again,
I ponder on the Fates that blow
Before a faithless wind.

'Twas once I thought I understood
The ways of life's great dream.
But, now I laugh to think how proud
And foolish I must seem
To all the gods who sit above
And watch the toils of man
And smile to think that one as I
Could hope to understand.

'Twas once I thought, as one would do,
Whose youth does still attend,
To weave in silk 'Le Passion Grand'
As weightless as the wind
And soar on enchanted wings.....
Ah, youth, you witless fool!
Better had you bent your strength
Upon some useful tool.

And plowed the fields for winter's store
Or sat before a loom,
For woven dreams of spider webs
Cannot dispel the gloom,
Nor fill the gut when famine strikes
And hunger gnaws your bones,
Nor warm you when the frost is thick
And finds you all alone.

Inconstant are the things of fluff,
The dreams of mortal man,
As changing as the listless clouds
That swirl and form again,
As fickle as the Fates that blow
Before a faithless wind
To tear apart the fabric of
The fragile dreams of men.

Spring Moon

What night is this when soaring moon,
Aglow with silent splendor,
Swells the empty heart and makes it
Eager for surrender?

No silver winter moon is this,
Nor amber autumn star,
Nor ever did the summer own
So glorious an orb

As this that soars above and stirs
The heart grown wintry cold,
Arousing embers, long thought dead,
To smolder, then burn bold.

Oh, vernal moon I know thee well,
Soft golden hawk in flight,
Were I still young and trusting I
Might welcome your sweet light.

But, I am old and know the truth of
Love's deceitful cruelty
And will not play the victim to your
Gentle argent beauty.

No childish dreamer am I now,
No feeble hopes remain,
For you to tease with faithless troth
And torture once again.

Such naïve dreams I once embraced,
While captured in your spell,
'Til wounded by a love that left
My heart an empty shell.

Oh, treacherous moon, release me now,
You auger me no boon,
But, yet would have me play the fool
And open all my wounds.

Oh, moon, I would not know the fire
Of love within my breast
Then feel the chilling emptiness
When love is put to test.

For love is but a fickle flame that
Dies when lust is sated
And leaves the grieving heart to weep,
Its trusting spirit jaded.

One More Summer's Day

When I am old with hopeless dreams,
Well worn and out of date,
Can I still turn to you, my Love,
And find you still my mate?
Will words so boldly spoken,
Without benefit of writ,
That bind us now together
Still remain as true and fixed
As when we first pronounced them,
In the height of youthful lust,
Or lie upon a cobwebbed shelf
Encased in layered dust?

How can I tell you of my fears
Without you think me weak?
And would you turn away from me
If I began to speak
Of daffodils in springtime bloom,
Their splendor soon to fade
To tarnished petals pressed between
The pages of yesterday;
Of autumn tugging at my sleeve,
With winter close behind,
And how the grey and shortened days
Cast shadows in my mind?

Or would you stay in sympathy
For one who's growing old
And cannot face the thought of being
Alone to face the cold?
Oh, Love, I could not bear to see
Such pity in your eyes,

Nor hear unspoken judgements
In the softness of your sighs.
'Tis better that I keep my fears
Concealed way deep inside
Then know, too soon, the moment when
Your love for me has died.

I'll show you only painted smiles
And never let you see
The aching pains inflicted by
My wild uncertainties.
I'll drink your wine and celebrate
Each day, one at a time,
And store up warmth against the day
Your sun no longer shines
Though fool I am to doubt you, I'm
Not fool enough to say,
For I would hold onto this dream
For one more summer's day.

To Know With Perfect Truth

Oh, for the anesthetic peace of sleep
To dream no dreams of ye
And to shed, for just the nonce,
These binding chains and free
My captured soul to rise aloft,
A splendor to the night
And softly smile in welcome to
The freedom of its flight.

As when, in youth and innocence,
It oft was wont to soar,
Unfettered by reality,
Unhampered nor unsure,
In search of one whose spirit song
Would match in harmony
And offer to the seeking heart
A warm security.

But, that was then and this is now
And youth has long since fled,
And the soul that would have gladly sung
Has never more than bled.
By unrequited passions flayed
And tossed 'pon lonely shores,
'Til time had left its hardened scars
Upon its fragile core.

Now, cruel my fated destiny,
I find, at last, too late
That one of whom the poets sing
And gods decree my fate.

That I should know such love in age
Too old to bind ye tight,
Except in dreams that fill my days
And rule my restless nights.

Would that I could shed the years
And set my spirit free,
For though I cannot bind ye, I
Am tightly bound to ye.
From this is come my twisting pain,
At once to hold and lose,
And know with perfect truth that I
Would ask and ye refuse.

Only The Wind

'Tis only the wind
That chills me face
And brings the tearing to me eyes;
'Tis only the wind, me lad,
'Tis only the wind
That sets me shoulders quaking.
And 'tis only the wind
That strikes me breast
And sends forth such doleful sighs,
'Tis only the wind, me lad,
'Tis only the wind
And not me heart a' breaking.

'Tis only the wind
That cast yer words
'Pon the storm that marks yer gaing;
'Tis only the wind, me lad,
'Tis only the wind
That toss the darkened clouds about.
And 'tis only the wind
That drops them now
On me, who will be staying
'Tis only the wind, me lad,
'Tis only the wind,
'Tis only the wind, no doubt.

It donna matter
That ye will gae
Or that ye ne'er return;
It donna matter, me lad,
It donna matter
That ye will quickly take ye're leave.

Aye, it donna matter
Sae don't ye fret
That yer words have caused me pain.
It donna matter, me lad,
It donna matter
For never have I loved ye.

'Twas only the wind
That screamed, ye see,
With a keening wail a'leaping;
'Twas only; the wind, me lad,
'Twas only the wind
That sweeps the craggy tor.
'Tis only the wind
That murmurs now
And sounds sae much like weeping;
'Tis only the wind, me lad,
The fell cold wind,
'Tis only the wind, nae more.

Upon The Lover's Bed

How do I speak when words alone
Are not enough to tell
Of ardent yearnings that come from where
The hungry heart does dwell?

Oh, I could say 'I love you'
For all that that would mean.
I say it to my mother
And, often, to my friends.
I could say to you 'I need you'
And that would mean no more,
For I've said it to too many souls
Too many times before.

And all the other words would mean
As much as those, you see,
For simple words cannot express
What stirs inside of me.

If only I could touch your flesh
And lay within your arms,
Then you would hear my restless soul
That's calling to your own.
That's when you'd know all that I feel
That never can be said
Until the day I lie with you
Upon the lover's bed.

Winter's Aging Bane

The sun, a pale and jaundiced eye,
Stares through the baleful clouds,
A warning of the storm to come
With winds that roar aloud.

Too soon, too soon, the hoary white
Of frost and snow appears
To strip us of our treasured warmth
And leave bare our racking fears.

Too well I know the bitter sting
Of winter's icy touch,
Too close I hold the memory
Of days once warmed from such.

What shelter shall avail me now,
What aegis from the cold?
Alone I watch the years pass by,
Each day, one day less bold.

When youthful fervor, burning zeal
And vigor warmed my blood,
Then rich the crops at harvest time
And filled the streams at flood.

But, now the wells are emptied dry
And sifting filtered sands,
Each grain in quick procession,
Pass through my trembling hands.

Cruel are the Fates that have decreed
No love should be fulfilled
From which to draw the warmth to stay
The fast approaching chill.

Too late to weep for youth that's spent,
Too little time remains,
In which to store against the blight
Of winter's aging bane.

Images

Gordie

Part I

Gordie, I hardly know ye, lad,
Though ye were once me mate,
When last I held your hand in mine
And walked ye to the gate.
Ye were off to war, me lad, and said ye would return.
Gordie, I waited for ye, lad,
These twenty years and some.

Yer hair is silver now, me lad,
Though once it were like gold,
And the fire that brightened up yer eyes
Has died and now grown cold.
Bent now the back I knew sae proud
And straight as e'er could be.
Gordie, I hardly know ye lad,
Ye've changed that much, ye see.

I hardly know ye, Gordie lad,
Though once I knew ye well,
And longed to hold yer hand in mine,
More than a lass can tell.
But, ye ne'er came back, Gordie lad,
Though I waited e'er so long.
Gordie, I don't want ye, lad,
Now ye have finally come.

What held ye, lad, that ye should wait
'Til I am old and worn?
Where did ye spend yer youth, me lad,
While me heart was pierced and torn?
Why come ye now when winter's ice

Has froze me old heart o'er?
Gordie, I hardly know ye, lad,
Ye've changed that much and more.

Gordie, I hardly know ye, lad,
Though once ye were me mate,
And I waited for ye, Gordie lad,
To walk back through that gate.
But, ye ne'er returned when war was done,
Not that year, nor any one.
Gordie, I donna went ye, lad.
Me love for ye is gone.

When ye left me, Gordie lad,
Yer bairn was in me womb.
But, I didn't worry o'er much,
Ye said ye'd be back soon.
I birthed him of a winter's night,
Bereft and all alone.
But, I waited for ye, Gordie lad,
Sae did yer own wee son.

I raised him up, the bonnie lad,
With eyes as blue as yers,
And a heart as pure as any man's,
Of that ye can be sure.
But, he had a need to know ye, lad,
When he was e'er sae young
And left to seek ye out, me lad,
When he became a man.

They brought him back, just yesterspring,
In a box hewn from an oak.
He never found ye, Gordie lad,
And his tender heart, it broke.
And now ye've come from whence ye were,

Although ye've come too late,
And I would not know ye, Gordie lad,
Nor let ye in me gate.

Gordie, I hardly know ye, lad,
Ye've changed and so have I.
I'm not the bonnie lassie that
Ye left alone to bide.
I waited for ye, Gordie lad,
These twenty years and some,
And now I will not have ye, lad.
Away with ye, be gone.

Part II

'Tis e'er so good to see ye, lass,
Ye're fair as e'er ye were
When I was such a foolish lad
And left ye for the war.
I had grand dreams of victory
And coming back sae proud.
But, that was not the way of it,
Though I fought well, I avow.

I saw the lads all strewn about
And covered o'er with gore
That shared me cup of uisqe beatha
On just the night afore.
Such stalwart lads as e'er were born
To Scotland and the clan,
Cut down by Harold's claymore, lass,
Their blood fed to the land.

I heard the wails and keening songs
Of those that did survive,
Mixed with the songs of triumph, lass,
Bought with their precious lives.

'Twas more than I could bear, sweet lass,
It broke me spirit sore,
And I could not come back home to ye,
Sae blooded by the war.
'Twas wounded that I was, me lass,
Though not by dirk, ye see,
And wounded did I spend me life
While I away from ye.
Sae many nights I've lain awake
And wished ye in me arms,
Or tossed about in froughten dreams
Of ye, all lost, forlorn.

I was filled with glamour dreams
And dinna ken, ye see,
That ye were breeding with me bairn
When I away from ye.
Or that I had a fine braw son,
With eyes like mine, ye say,
Until I met with ye, me lass,
Upon this vera day.

'Tis sorry that I am, me lass,
That I left ye all alone,
And sorry more I dinna know
The lad who was me own.
And sorry still I come too late
To save you from such pain,
For ye were e'er me dearling fair
And I would not be yer bane.

For all that I deserted ye
And wandered long afar,
Ne'er did I forget ye, lass,
Nor cease to love ye hard.
But, I've caused ye so much woe, sweet lass,

And would not cause ye more,
So I will be away and cast
No shadow on your door.

Part III

Och, Gordie, do not leave me, lad,
I cannot see ye go,
Nor let ye think I donna care
About ye any more.
'Twas pain that spoke and not me heart,
Oh, no, 'tis not too late.
Come in, me lad, I've waited long
And will not close the gate.

Old Man, Early Winter

Seated in a row of haunted eyes
That stare out of haunted faces,
His eyes wandered about
The leaf-strewn lawn.
"Looks like an early winter
This year", he said.
"Not much to do these days
But watch the wind
Scatter the dry leaves about
And listen to the creaking
Of the old rocker chairs.
Old! But, not always.
And not always so tired, either.
There was a time once.....
But, then, that was long ago
And the memory ain't too clear.
Still, there was a time.....
Somewhere, back there
In the back of my mind,
There's the ghost of a memory
That keeps niggling at me,
Just a whisper
Brought up by a pretty girl's smile
Or the tinkle of laughter
Floating on the air,
Just a whisper, nagging
Like an old crone wife.
Funny how those things
Just don't want to die.
Like me.
I don't want to die.
It's times, when I almost remember,

That I think I might live a while longer,
Times when the ghost
Comes plucking at my sleeve,
Distant skirls of music,
Fragrant traces of lilac
Drifting on the air
With the dreams of youth.
Marty started it all, you know,
With his constant humming
Tunes from the twenties and thirties
That most other folks never heard
And, if they did,
They don't remember.
Marty remembers.
Marty hums a lot,
Most all the time.
Don't do no good, complaining.
We all done that,
One time or another,
And it ain't made no difference.
None at all.
He still hums.
One of them tunes,
Can't place the name to it,
Is what brung up that ghost.
Can't place the name
To much these days.
Marty remembers.
Smells like snow.
Going to be an early winter this year,
An early winter."

El Toro

His head thrown back,
Eyes burning black
From the stench of blood and gore,
Still breathing hard,
He stands his guard
O're the dying matador.

His blood undried
From injured side,
Glistens darkly on the sword.
Viewed with disdain,
It lies unclaimed
By the dying matador.

The shame once borne,
The echoed scorn,
The cries, 'matar el toro'
Begin to fade,
The dues now paid
By the dying matador.

"'Tis Tommy this, and Tommy that
And kick him out, the brute,
But, 'tis savior of his country
When the guns begin to shoot."
Rudyard Kipling

Tommy

He heard the guns again today,
Staccato burst within his brain,
Enemies firing through the rain,
No place to hide, no time to pray,
He heard the guns again today.

He saw his friends again today,
Shattered bodies washed in gore,
Scattered o'er the jungle floor,
Dead eyes stare in stark dismay,
He saw his friends again today.

His children call from day to day,
Thirteen years since they moved away,
They call to ask 'are you okay?'
Especially when it starts to rain,
That's when he hears the guns again.

He heard the guns again today,
Screaming in a tortured mind,
Horrid sounds not left behind,
The price returning soldiers pay,
To hear the guns, day after day.

The Emigrant Brook

Born of the mountain,
Her soft waters fed,
Freshly and coolly,
From the green dragon's head,
She sings as she plays
In her birthplace of hills
But, silently she courses
Her path through the fields.

Yesterday's Child

Curling tendrils of hickory smoke
Rise above the trees,
To blend with cotton puffs of clouds
And drift upon the breeze.

In winter camp among the firs,
Where bough and branch conceal,
A trapper sits mid furs and truck
And cooks his evening meal.

Dressed in skins and blanket coat,
His flintlock gun at hand,
He tells a tale, in graphic scene,
Of the ancient mountain man;

Of autumn nights and spring filled days
And summer rendezvous;
Of years of walking God's own land
Bought with the beaver plews;

Of mountain lakes and valley ponds
And ice encrusted streams
Where a man could pull the pelts to pay
For one more season's dream;

Of a man who dreams of walking paths
That long ago grew o'er
And a weekend spent among these hills
Filled with the mountain's lore.

Curling tendrils of hickory smoke
Rise in the mountain cold
To drift above the winter camp
Of yesterday's child below.

The Omen

The dragon stirs
Beneath its hills,

The sparrow's heart flutters,
For a moment, then stills,

The shivering fox
Hides in her lair,

But, the trader continues
To trade, unaware.

Autumn

Redolent gardens
And gentle fall nights,
Moonlight depicting
The snow geese in flight,
That call on the chill wind
Their tales of the north,
Of winter that follows
And fires at the hearth.

Jars full of cider
And bare apple trees,
Splitting up firewood
And raking up leaves,
Ghosties and goblins
And scarecrows galore,
Cornstalks and pumpkins
And putting up stores.

Hayrides on wagons
And barns filled with hay,
Roasting up chestnuts
At end of the day,
Cawing of crows
And barking of dogs,
Fireflies that flicker
And singing tree frogs.

Women's Song

Old women sit in circle form
As flames reflect from breast and arm,
Oiled flesh aglow while softly moan,
Their anguished voice in chanted drone,
Their sorrow songs on smoke arise
To still the breath of battle cries,
For warriors borne by brothers bold
To waiting arms of sisters, cold,
Their praises sung to fathers' ears,
Their bodies washed by mothers' tears.
Young women sit in circle form
And weep for sons as yet unborn.

Summer Watch

He sits within the stillness, waiting.
Surrounded by a cacophony of birdsong,
Soothed by the gentle murmur
Of a babbling stream,
Embraced by the warmth
Of the solstice sun,
He sits within his sanctuary
And holds his silent vigil.
Above him sheltering hemlocks sigh
And sycamores rustle in the breeze,
All around him small creatures play
While he sits, waiting,
Undeterred that no one comes,
He waits, as he has waited
Each solstice,
Throughout the years.

Trail's End

(On the Cherokee Trail of Tears)

On feet that had
Long ago lost all feeling,
She plodded barefoot
Through the snow,
The soldiers' bayonets
At her back,
Driving her, ever westward,
Into the setting sun.
At her breast she carried
The cold body of her infant son
She was unable to abandon
Along the trail.
She takes it with her,
A guardian to his spirit.
So many gone ahead,
So many more to follow.
A frozen sparrow
Fell dead at her feet.
She accepted its tiny burden
As one more gentle spirit
To escort home,
Into the west,
Into the spirit world.

Rendezvous Midnight

(A mountain man's song)

The last of the campfires
Still glows in the night,
Sending out probing
Fingers of light
That dance in the shadows
And seek out the eyes
Of small furry creatures
That hurry to hide.

While spirits, who walk
In the soft autumn air,
Call forth the night hunters
From den and from lair.
The cry of a hoot owl
Hushes the murmur
Of those who have not yet
Gone to their slumber.

A skitter, a scurry,
A sigh on the breeze,
A fluttering stir
Of dry autumn leaves,
The smile of a dreamer,
Asleep in his furs,
Alive in his visions
But, dead to the world.

The whisper of water,
The croak of a frog
Who's holding his court
At the base of a log.

It's rendezvous midnight,
A magical hour,
When the moon soars high
And man's dreams even higher.

All the world has gone quiet
And peacefully still,
While the lingering embers
Hold back the night chill.
A time when thoughts wander,
Here and there as they may,
While you savor the events
Of the preceding day.

And breathe in the history
Of a primitive camp
As seen in the darkness
By a quarter moon's lamp.

Summer Clouds

He spent his years in free pursuit
Of drifting summer clouds
And sang his songs of joy and pain
And wonderment, aloud.

He spent his tears and smiles the same
And never gave them thought,
Nor ever once considered that,
Perhaps, he even aught.

He shared his love, his only wealth,
He's known both rain and sun,
And never looked to trace his path
From whence it first begun.

He set his foot each day to chase
The noblest cloud he saw
And winked at passing strangers who
Would never hear the call.

Lazy, drifting summer clouds,
He's followed you to here
And lived a life as rich and full
As any on this sphere.

With no regrets, no looking back,
No counting up the score,
He took firm hold of wispy dreams
And headed out the door.

And now, when winter's ice and snow
Have grounded him the while,
He often thinks, in reverie,
Of summer clouds and smiles.

The Winds of Time

Where go the blooms
That flower then do fall,
Their fragrance scattered on the wind,
Their petals on the wall?

Where go the leaves
That fly before the wind,
Forsaking trees that, naked, stand
As omens to old men?

Where go the years
That are so quick to fly
And leave so little of themselves
As they go passing by?

Whence comes theses winds,
Where does their birthplace lie?
Where do they carry earth's debris,
Those living things that die?

Circus Clowns

Long ago and far away,
In a land where joy abounds,
There lived a boy, in innocence,
Who loved the circus clowns.
He watched them dance and chase about
And laughed until he cried.
No matter that they always lost,
He loved the way they tried.

But, he grew up and they did not
And he left the land behind
To take up lonely residence
In a much, much different kind,
Where they destroy your will to strive,
Or even hope for more,
And crush your, oh, so fragile dreams
Like petals on the floor.

A bitter land of crippled psyches,
Of egos bruised and scarred,
Where windows op'ning to the soul are
Carefully locked and barred.
No laughing, dancing circus clowns
To cheer you on to win.
To laugh, to dance, to struggle on
Evokes the scorn of men.

Assailed by a hostile culture
With twisted ecstasies,
His healthy boyhood faith slain by
A malignant Judasy,
He fought with all the strength he had
To keep his dreams alive.

But, with no clowns to comfort him,
He slowly died inside.

He took a stoic's visage in
Surrender to his fate.
No one can ever touch him now,
He's learned to compensate,
But, late at night, when he's alone,
When no one is around,
He dares to risk a smile as he
Remembers circus clown

The Oracle

September's breeze
Excites the trees
And whispers to the sparrow,
Go gather there
Where sleeps the hare
Mid sage and golden yarrow.

With den of bear
And fox's lair
And eagle's aerie warm
You'll find the peace
Your spirit seeks
And shelter from the storm.

Uttered Nonsense

Heralds

The honks of wild geese on the wing,
Announce the coming of the spring,
Echoed by the cawing crows
And an owl that hoots,
I told you so,
I told you so,
Spring is come, I told you so.

Madder Gnatters

Have you ever seen a madder gnatter?
I've seen one, you know.
The more a madder gnatter bites
The madder the gnatter grows.

They'll bite you on an arm or leg
Or on your tender neck
Why, they'll bite you any place that
Isn't covered, I suspect.

Not only do they bite you but,
They expect that you should listen
While they drone on endlessly
Of how well and true they've bitten.

Madder gnatters love to boast
Of just how madder they can get,
They're even known to speculate,
To wager and to bet.

Every summer all the gnatters
Meet at a convention
To settle all their postulations,
Their claims and their contentions.

All the gnatters are mad, of course,
But, some are madder than the rest,
And it's a madder gnatters' picnic
When they meet to choose the best.

With every single bite they take,
They get a little madder,
Until they find out which one is
The maddest of all the gnatters.

They bite and bite until they find
The maddest gnatter of them all,
And then they crown him gnatter king
And throw a gnatter ball.

I knew a madder gnatter once who
Set out to bite a page.
He bit and bit and bit until
He exploded in a rage.

I've seen madder gnatters madder
Than a hatter, and that's a fact.
But, I've never seen a gnatter madder
Than the one that I bit back.

The Ins and Outs of Importance

I have a tale of great import
But, before I can begin,
I have to let my dear cat out
And bring my dog back in.
This I really have to do
Before he bothers kitty,
For he will snap and snarl and scrap
And never will take pity.

Now, where was I? Oh, yes, I know,
Something dire I must relate.
I know it is important
But, it just will have to wait
Until I let the dog back out
And bring the kitty in.
Not to let the doggy run
Would be a horrid sin.

I'm sure that what I have to say
Is important and all that
But, how can I expect to think
When bothered by the cat,
Who's fussing to be let out,
And the dog, to be let in?
Oh, I'm sure to tell you soon enough
But, you'll have to wait 'til then.

Oh, dear! Oh, my! For goodness sake,
There is no need to shout.
After I bring the poor cat in
And let the poor dog out,
I'll tell you all about it,
It's a sordid tale, it's true.

All I need is time to give
The regard that it is due.

Why do you go? Please sit back down,
You really must not leave.
After I tell you what I've heard,
I'm sure you will agree
That it's worth waiting for,
There truly is no doubt.
Well, if you must, bring in the dog
And let the cat back out.

The Saga of Hamish Spoor Hunter

(A true and faithful accounting)

'Twas the first day of the season,
A fine and frisky day,
But when old Hamish finally woke
It was well upon its way.

He rushed about in frenzied haste,
'I've got to get my deer'
We heard him cry when gravel flew
As he sped away from here.

Now, Mom and I, we waited,
Sure of his marksman shot.
We knew that the he would not return
'Til he had bagged his lot.

So, when we saw his car approach
And pull up to the ramp
We figured one was hanging
Down at the Southpaw camp.

We braced ourselves with freezer wrap
And butcher knife at hand.
We wouldn't stop until the steaks
Were sizzling in the pan.

He looked at us with saddened eyes,
Tinged with a hint of fear.
'You won't be needing all of that.
I didn't get my deer.'

He braced his shoulders for the pain
And stood up like a man.
'I shot, before it could escape,
The window out the van'.

'But, what about our venison
Our steaks, our ribs, our roasts?
And what about that fine backstrap
Our tummies love the most?'

He smiled a very knowing smile
And brightened up a bit.
He reached into his pocket
And bade us both to sit.

Then, with a victor's flourish,
He opened up his hand
To show to us a chunk of spoor,
The biggest in the land.

With pride he grabbed his hunter's guide,
That good and faithful book.
And, pointing to a chart, he said,
'Now just you take a look.'

'This book', he said, 'is proof to all,
For doubt I know they would,
This spoor came from the biggest buck
To walk these north Maine woods!'

Two wardens stopped to say hello
And one RCMP.
He trotted out his pride and joy
And passed it 'round with glee.

Out came his book with trusted chart,
His calipers and rule.
'Just see that size, it goes to prove
Old Hamish is no fool.

Then turning to the warden, he
Said with shoulders squared,
'Now, tag it Sir, you'll never find
One bigger anywhere.

'I plan to mount my spoor and want
The tag to prove my claim
That when it comes to hunting I'm
The best sport in the game.

With that he set about to clean
Debris from out the car
Assured that soon his fame would spread
To all, both near and far.

Bring out the pipes, let's dance a jig,
We'll celebrate his fame.
Hamish, hunter of the spoor,
They'll not forget your name!

Marcus's Song

He's Marcus the cat
And that's where it's at,
A very uncommon feline,
He goes for a jog
With a little white dog
And plays until it's bedtime.

Then, he cuddles another
He thinks is his brother,
Why this is, I really don't know,
But, he sleeps in their bed
And eats what they're fed
And follows wherever they go.

They seem to agree,
He's their cup of tea,
They're happy to have him along,
'Cause, he's Marcus the cat
And that's where it's at
And this is his own special song.

Scooter's Song

He wants his loving everyday
And he wants it every night,
He wants his loving, he's a lover
And wants to taste delight.

He has a cat who adores him and a mama
Who loves him more than anyone can ever do.

He likes to howl at the moon,
To bay and to croon,
He's a darling, he's a sweetheart,
He's my precious little Scooter Maldoon.

Chester's Song

He wakes up every morning
With a busy day ahead,
There's a yard full of chickens
That are better off as dead,
There's a cat to torment
And plans to foment
And a million things to do
Before it's time to go to bed.

He's an angel in the parlor
But, a devil in the hall,
He chases all the cars
And never comes when Mama calls.
But, he's Daddy's little boy,
His one and only joy,
So, I guess we have to keep
The little Chester after all.

Tedward's Song

He's the Tedward Aloysius
And he's known to be officious.
He has a haughty attitude,
He's arrogant and rude,
He's the pompous little Tedward Aloysius.

He's the Tedward Aloysius
And often is contentious.
When he gloms onto a bone
You'd better leave the boy alone,
He's a feisty little Tedward Aloysius.

He's the Tedward Aloysius,
He's loud and he's vociferous.
He makes his wishes know
With barks to make you groan,
He's demanding is our Tedward Aloysius.

He's the Tedward Aloysius,
He's brazen and audacious,
He struts about the yard
Expecting an award,
He's the shameless little Tedward Aloysius.

He's the Tedward Aloysius
And I think he'd be delicious.
Though just a tiny shih tzu,
If you cooked him in a stew,
He'd make a tasty little Tedward Aloysius.

Limericks

I wrote a most glorious song.
I wrote it both quickly and long.
'Twas easily wrote,
It had but one note
And 'twas writ to be played on a gong.

Why the dog was wearing a muzzle
To no one was much of a puzzle.
'Twas not done in fun,
But, to keep him from rum
Which he was bound, by habit, to guzzle.

I once taught my fingers to tat,
Then I tatted the hair on a gnat.
When the gnat was all done,
I said, 'oh, what fun',
And started right in on the cat.

I once caught a frog on a log,
And another from out of the bog.
I sautéed them up nice
And mixed them with rice,
And offered them both to my dog.

Index

About the Author

J. S. T. Botting is of Cherokee descent. She lives on a home farm in the hills of West Virginia with her husband, cat and three dogs. Poetry is, and always has been, her passion. She does not always follow a strict poetic form but, instead, lets the words flow as they come from somewhere deep inside of her. She started writing at the age of twelve and had numerous poems from those early years published in magazines and periodicals. Later in life she belonged to a group of poets in upstate New York who read their works in an open forum. Her efforts there were well received and often acclaimed by the attending public. She draws her inspiration from people and creatures that she refers to as her muses or by something she has seen or read. All of her poems reflect a deep understanding of both animal and human emotions and, in some cases, a whimsical appreciation of the absurd.

Printed in the United States
By Bookmasters